Praise About the Author

As a university professor who has literally read and evaluated thousands of papers and manuscripts, I can recommend Jeana's book to you. Rather than providing an abstract approach of what could be, Jeana proves that her method works. Her approach is straightforward: pick a target, assemble the right team, and then execute the plan to achieve victory. Refreshingly, she insists that we must be led by guiding principles to achieve a greater good. You will learn to win and achieve your own goals by embracing Jeana's wisdom. Reading and studying her book is worth it.

William D. Danko, Ph.D.
Coauthor of *The Millionaire Next Door* and *Richer Than A Millionaire: A Pathway To True Prosperity*

At the heart of business success is value. If you want to win, you have to be worth it. Jeana has figured out how to do just that: build a business that is worth it. Now, she's sharing her strategy. **WORTH IT** *is a priceless guide to modern-day leadership and boundless success.*

Gino Wickman
Author of *Traction* and Creator of EOS Worldwide

Jeana's rise as a professional has been inspirational, and her book feels like a roadmap to success.

Lance Morgan
CEO Ho-Chunk Inc. & Founding Partner of Big Fire Law & Policy Group

In Worth It, Jeana Goosmann quickly gets real about an entrepreneur's journey and delivers a powerful message to the reader that is consistent with her winning leadership style and personality. Readers will feel the experience of Jeana's journey and be able to clearly adapt ideas, concepts, best practices for their own. Simply stated it's worth it to read "Worth It".

Boyd Ober
President & CEO
Author-Magnitude: Releasing the Power of Your Leadership Presence

Jeana's book, "Worth It" includes a number of her guiding principles that she has set in motion in both her personal and professional life. As a business entrepreneur, attorney, and philanthropist, it's great to have these highlighted so others can aspire for similar effectiveness and business success.

Jennifer McCabe, CBIS
President & CEO
Opportunities Unlimited

Jeana Goosmann and her book "Worth It" is a must read for people who desire success in business. As a leader in a law firm myself that works with high net worth clients I recommend her R.E.D. philosophy if you want to drive results.

Jonathan E. Gopman, Esquire
Chair, Trusts & Estates Practice Akerman LLP

I'm so impressed with Jeana Goosmann's guide to being a successful leader and entrepreneur. As an author, attorney and CEO, Jeana knows how to launch and grow a thriving business and through sharing personal stories about her life, her family and her challenges along the way, she intimately illustrates how you can be Ready, Execute and Deliver the kind of career that not just exceeds expectations but shatters them! Read Worth It...it's, well, worth it!

Lisa Guerrero
Chief Investigative Correspondent
Inside Edition

Jeana Goosmann lights up a room. Her enthusiasm for business is only outshined by her brains and kindness. **WORTH IT** *is the modern-day business person's playbook for success.*

Mary Ann O'Brien
CEO & Founder of OBI Creative

I had the privilege of being Jeana's business coach for over two years. I learned to never underestimate the power of her dreams and her resolve to make them happen. She has the unique ability to communicate bold goals that inspire others to participate in making them happen. R.E.D. is her manifesto, and she's #worthit!

Mark Ellsworth
Former Managing Partner of Cain Ellsworth & Company CPA firm and Vistage CEO Board Chair

I've had the pleasure of working with both Jeana and her team over the last several years, both personally and with clients. The mantra of R.E.D. is clearly apparent in how they operate—ready, execute, and deliver. Whether it is a presentation or a client investment project, with Goosmann's guidance I am ready to execute and deliver at the top levels, resulting in a satisfied audience and client. I'm intrigued to see where Jeana and her team go next!

Mike Ridder
Owner, Blueprint Business Advisory

Jeana Goosmann and her firm have made a huge splash in several of our markets. They are progressive, forward thinking, and are changing the law firm model itself. They have gone from a relatively small, unknown firm to seemingly everywhere. Their introductions to several manufacturing and services firms have been invaluable.

Mike Anderson
Managing Director at Bridgepoint Investment Banking

*Jeana Goosmann offers brilliant advice for today's leaders and entrepreneurs. I will recommend **WORTH IT** to anyone with purpose, drive, and desire to be successful. **WORTH IT** is very refreshing. The R.E.D. philosophy will contribute not only to the success of entrepreneurs, it will also benefit established business leaders. I will implement the Ready, Execute, Deliver mindset in my current business to increase my market share. **WORTH IT** has opened up my creativity to do more by concentrating on what is important and letting go of what is not.*

*I wholeheartedly support the lessons that Jeana outlines in **WORTH IT**!*

Van Deeb
Author and CEO of DEEB Companies

Jeana's entrepreneurial spirit is infectious.

Heath Kooiman
CPA Woltman Group

I had the unique experience of starting an intellectual property law firm around the same time Jeana started the Goosmann Law Firm. From that experience, Jeana's business acumen was readily apparent, and her success is a testament to her ability to execute on an ambitious growth strategy. In addition, her ability to build her business while maintaining a "MashUp" strategy is a great example of insight for blending all aspects of life to fuel an environment for a business to flourish.

Ryan Grace
Owner and Founding Partner of Advent LLP law firm

Jeana is someone who practices what she preaches! Her R.E.D. Philosophy: Ready, Execute, and Deliver works!! I've seen it in action as her client for 15 years as I've asked her to handle a WIDE variety of challenging and complex corporate and personal legal needs. She's DELIVERED in every situation in and out of the courtroom. She proudly wears the color red daily and has the color throughout her law offices as a reminder of her winning philosophy to consistently WOW her clients!

Brad Pinchuk
President and Chief Executive Officer of Hirschbach Motor Lines

I was catching up on my local business magazines when I ran across an article in Strictly Business about Jeana Goosmann. I enjoyed reading the fact that she was newer to the Omaha scene and the impact she wanted to make with her law firm. I knew I needed to meet her because of her connection with local business, which is a passion of mine. Coincidentally, while looking her up, Jeana had just moved her firm across the street from our Berkshire Hathaway HS offices. Coincidental or destined? My Activator strength took over. I called her office and arranged a meet and greet. Jeana did not disappoint. She is true to herself, her team, and her place in the community. We have since sent reciprocal referrals, and I will continue to do so going forward. I'm pleased to be her colleague, acquaintance, and friend. I can't wait to be a part of the future with her.

Wendy Richey
Director of Business Acquisitions, Sales & Consulting
Berkshire Hathaway/Ambassador
Commercial Division

My experience with Jeana and her team at Goosmann Law has been exceptional. We've engaged attorneys in important matters at Hope Haven and I've used one personally as well. Excellence is woven into their culture from the top down. Goosmann Law has elevated the support and protection of our mission to serve thousands of people with disabilities each year, and we're proud to work with them.

Matt Buley
Chief Executive Officer of Hope Haven

I believe who you are in business with matters. Your partners/providers can either make or break your ability to achieve your goals! Jeana Goosmann and her team have proven to be a powerful alliance. Always on point, always responsive and accurate in their advice means challenges are addressed professionally and effectively! Having the best "on your side" makes all the difference! Thank you Jeana and team!

Kacy Bell
Operating Principle of Keller Williams Realty

Fun, easy, and informative read. Especially enjoyed how Jeana breaks down the different facets of business and working with clients through the R.E.D. philosophy!

Ryan J. Miller
Financial Advisor and Shareholder Renaissance Financial

*If you're going to pour your heart, sweat, and life savings into a business, then you better have the right guide. Jeana Goosmann makes **WORTH IT** worth it!*

Jeffrey Hayzlett
Primetime TV & Radio Host, Speaker, Author and Part-Time Cowboy

Jeana Goosmann is a true visionary in entrepreneurial leadership! She has an uncanny ability to transform a complacent business environment into an action-oriented leadership organization that is destined to perform at its best and achieve positive results. Her coaching and mentoring has sparked new energy and vibrancy into our organization from the first time I met Jeana, and it continues to this day.

Daniel Wolfe, J.D., Ph.D.,
Senior Vice President, DecisionQuest

Jeana is an outstanding "connector" of people and opportunities. She introduced us to a business opportunity that has turned into a highly strategic component of our overall business. Her high energy, creativity, and strategic focus have benefited our business immensely, and we have been blessed to work with her!

Dennis Johnson
President, Ho-Chunk Real Estate

WORTH IT is a concise, compelling read that propels you forward into action. Jeana Goosmann uses engaging personal anecdotes and relatable examples to illustrate how to attack the hurdles we face in life and at work, and her R.E.D. framework provides a powerful tool that orients the reader toward engagement and results. It's a worthwhile read for the seasoned leader and for those on the rise that want to sharpen their edge with insight, momentum, and self-confidence.

Ted Gavin
Managing Director & Founding Partner at Gavin/Solmonese LLC

At last, a book for emerging women business leaders from someone who is actually a successful woman in business. I am thrilled to recommend Jeana Goosmann's new book, WORTH IT. This book is an inspiring, go-to guide for the woman who is ready to take massive action to create her own destiny. This is a fun, easy-to-read book that explores the mindset and the skills required to become a great leader. Jeana is a gifted storyteller and has the moxie and business acumen to back it up. She is truly a SmartFem. I highly recommend WORTH IT.

Lea Woodford
CEO of SmartFem Media Group

WORTH IT

WORTH IT

BUSINESS LEADERS:
READY. EXECUTE. DELIVER.

JEANA GOOSMANN
THE CEO'S ATTORNEY

THRONE
PUBLISHING GROUP

Throne Publishing Group
2329 N Career Ave #215
Sioux Falls, SD 57107
ThronePG.com

Visit www.beworthit.com for information on our conferences and workshops.

Explore www.goosmannlaw.com for legal resources and to contact the firm.

Table of Contents

PART THREE: DELIVER

Introduction

Are you building something that is worth the sacrifice? Worth the early mornings and late nights? Worth the bumps, scrapes, and bruises? Are you leading a business and life that are truly *worth everything you are pouring in*?

These questions drive me and color my entire organization. *Worth It* is so much more than a book title or catchphrase; it's the mantra of our practice. What can we do to ensure we are always *worth it*? As leaders, this goes even deeper than our business, culture, and client experience.

Every day, we have to show up and be someone who is worth following. When everything is on the line, can we perform at our highest level? Can we develop and execute the strategies that let us walk away from the negotiation table with exactly what we wanted? More importantly, are we building a thriving business *and* life?

I wrote this book to share the strategies and mindsets that help me answer, and embody, these questions every day: The R.E.D. Philosophy. R.E.D. means *ready, execute,* and *deliver.* It serves as a simple, but wildly powerful, framework for peak performance and high-impact leadership.

READY: Winning is built on a foundation of preparation and always being ahead of your competition.

EXECUTE: Vision becomes reality by implementing carefully crafted plans and building a world-class team that can execute.

DELIVER: Results go to those who are *all in* and believe every goal is within reach.

Are you ready to execute, deliver, and build a life and business that's worth it?

R.E.D. Philosophy

R.E.D. leaders build lives and businesses
that are always *worth it.*
You are READY.
You have put in the time. Everything before
has prepared you for this moment.
You will EXECUTE.
You take action. Your plan is impeccable;
now it's time to turn it into reality.
You always DELIVER.
Your favorite place is in the ring. You hit
and exceed the mark.

PART ONE

READY

READY. EXECUTE. DELIVER.

CHAPTER 1

R.E.D. Foundation

Entrepreneurship isn't a job for which you send in a résumé. It doesn't come with a guaranteed paycheck. Loyal employees aren't part of the package. What does come with entrepreneurship is risk, uncertainty, fear, and *really* challenging, uncharted waters to navigate. Honestly, I wouldn't have it any other way. True entrepreneurs are in a class of their own; not only because they're special, but also because they have to be able to make it. They leave comfort behind through courage, focus, and ingenuity.

Having worked with countless business leaders and entrepreneurs during the past two decades, I've discovered five key attributes foundational to successful entrepreneurs. The soil from which they grow is enriched with qualities I call "entrepreneurial DNA." Although they're expressed differently depending upon context, they're the elements that build thriving, sustainable, and wildly successful companies.

The best entrepreneurs inspire and achieve by being bold, confident, strong, and visionary as they become activators.

Trait 1: Boldness

Bold entrepreneurs shine when everything is on the line. They are willing to take risks when others are not. They're willing to be the first, because they know that leading often means stepping out before the path looks safe. Boldness sets them apart, because when others question what they're doing, they're resolute in their belief that they will make it happen.

When fear of failure and the unknown lurk, real entrepreneurs jump anyway. They understand that listening to fear will simply trap their ideas in their head. Stepping out in boldness captures their moment through action. Bold entrepreneurs never say, "I wish I would have . . ." in regret. Big results belong to the bold.

Trait 2: Confidence

An entrepreneur's boldness creates confidence, which I define as ultimate conviction in one's own thoughts and beliefs. Confidence builds a steel backbone that won't be broken. After all, how can someone take great risks if they don't unequivocally believe in their ideas and plans?

Not only does confidence prompt bold moves, but it also engenders faith in the entrepreneur. You're not a leader unless somebody follows. But nobody wants to follow someone they don't believe in. Confidence is required to sell the idea, the mission, and the vision.

Trait 3: Strength

All of the confidence in the world won't prevent adversity. Everything worth doing is met with difficulty, which is why real entrepreneurs are strong. They are powerful enough to punch through the hard times. This is especially true when they're the first ones to try something. Maybe it's a new business model no one is sure will work. Maybe it's an untested market into which they're going to expand. Or maybe it's a radically different kind of product, service, or company.

An entrepreneur without this internal strength will crumble beneath the pressure and self-doubt. Their work will collapse, because it takes strength to keep from imploding when you're the only one who sees potential where everyone else sees nothing but risk. This strength is what makes them exactly the right people to do great things.

Trait 4: Visionary

Henry Ford has been credited with this adage: "If I had asked people what they wanted, they would have said faster horses."

Where people saw only incremental improvement upon the status quo, Ford saw a new class entirely—the automobile. This perfectly illustrates the fourth trait and strand of the DNA possessed by true entrepreneurs: vision.

Entrepreneurs with vision will have a solid grasp on the overall picture of their plans, but also will understand that there will be hurdles. Taking hold of a vision means you are more than a dreamer—you can see the end result and anticipate the difficulties in getting there.

The path is illuminated and requires both a plan and action steps. What is the driving force? Accountability—write it down and commit. This plays itself out every day. For instance, when opportunities arise that are outside the end goals, they have to wait. Visionary entrepreneurs have the discernment and wisdom to understand that saying "no" to projects or work that distracts from the end goal is as important as saying "yes" to what moves the project forward.

Trait 5: Activation

The fifth trait brings them all together, creating the sort of mythic figure who can disrupt entire industries. I call this DNA trait activation. An activator is the person who jumps into the pool—clothes on, shoes filling with water, all by themselves, without being paralyzed by fear of what others think. An activator walks the talk.

Activators get the ball rolling because their hands are not tied by uncertainty. They are confident and can back up what they *say* because of what they *do*.

Activators simply stand out. People who live on the sidelines are stuck in their heads—running on a hamster wheel while rehearsing all the reasons the vision won't come to pass. To them, the obstacles are larger than the possibilities.

An activator lays the groundwork, establishes the plan, executes, fills the gap when something falls short, and does it over and over again. They are in the game because they believe it's better to play, and play to win, than to sit on the sidelines. They have the end game set in their hearts, and they lead their team with the conviction to achieve.

A Legacy of Entrepreneurial DNA

I didn't pull these entrepreneurial traits from thin air or pluck them from the pages of a textbook. They came from somewhere far deeper: real-world experience. I've watched them work and unfold my entire life and career. It all started with my parents.

My father, Frank Seitzinger, was an entrepreneur and farmer in northwest Iowa. He was incredibly resilient—the guy who jumped into the deep end of the pool with both cowboy boots on, unfazed by what "normal" folks did. This drove him to be one of the first in Iowa to take on no-till farming, earning him a reputation for innovation. And that's the lesson here: great entrepreneurs always dare to be the first. They don't wait for permission or for someone else to take the lead. This is how my father lived and did business.

By the time I was born, my father owned a 10,000-acre farm in northern Minnesota called the Klondike, had built a new house on the property, and flew his private plane to business deals across the country. How did he get there? Because of his entrepreneurial DNA.

Put On Your Big Deal Boots

Now, imagine a cowboy-turned-businessman stepping out of his private plane wearing snake- and alligator-skin boots. This was my father, and he called them his "big deal boots." I've realized that we, as entrepreneurs, need to put on our big deal boots, too. What in the heck are they?

My father always wore them to make the big-figure deals. They were his personal symbol that it was time for big business, and he was showing up to win. I'm not saying we all need to pick up a pair of striking alligator-skin boots, but we need to assume that attitude of boldness and posture of confidence.

Beyond the boots, my father was a powerful negotiator and a man to be taken seriously. It was his knowledge, talent, and perseverance that made him bold in his decision-making. This helped him grow a farming operation that included a grain warehouse bigger than the local mall. He would eventually sell the Klondike farm. In his foresight—*or entrepreneurial vision*—he retained the right of first refusal to buy back the land. This proved extremely lucrative, as he did eventually buy it back.

When I think of an activator who dives in without looking back, I see my father. He was always *doing*. He had a voracious appetite for reading and learning. He took seriously the technological advances of his time and embraced innovation. In short, he never let a big deal, idea, or opportunity sit unexecuted.

Expect Bumps in the Road

Even for all his action, my father also taught me to be kind, generous, and wise, the traits of a business person who can see a vision and scale it without stepping on others to get there. He took care of his employees, volunteered locally, and took seriously the idea that his success, and the success of those around him, created a stronger community.

My father's impact is both metaphorical and literal. There is a bump in the interstate between Sioux City, Iowa, and Omaha, Nebraska, where the rail line travels beneath the road. It's a sweet reminder to me every time I drive over that swell in the road that my father had a hand in getting the rail line to come to the farm to transport grain because of his business's enormous scale. Was it hard for him to build something so large and successful? Yes. Was it worth it? Absolutely.

True entrepreneurs expect bumps in the road with the understanding that they will eventually become landmarks to our success.

Do What It Takes

My father was an incredible entrepreneur, but my mother, Bonnie, was at his side every step of the way. She created her own waves as a leader who had a knack for making people feel like they were important, no matter where they came from or where they were going. She was the chief networker and lived by the premise that success is not worth it if you're not helping others.

As the Queen of the Daughters of the Nile, a women's organization that is part of the Shriners, she spent hours cooking peanut brittle with friends to benefit a children's burn unit in Texas. As much a mover and shaker in philanthropy as my father was in business, she sold 800 boxes in one year! The brittle was made at the Shriners' temple, but that year it was too humid and the sugar was getting too sticky to stay at the temple. So, the operation moved into our home—I can still see the basement stacked high with white boxes of peanut brittle.

There was an entrepreneurial spirit in my mother as well that resonated during my childhood. On a mission to make more, to do more for those injured kids, she bought ingredients in bulk to lower the price and leveraged a connection with the largest ice cream manufacturer in the world to get the best prices to improve the margin.

My mother *showed* me that entrepreneurs do whatever it takes. If we have to bring the peanut brittle home and keep it in the basement to make it fly, then that's what we do! Why? Because entrepreneurs see the vision and hold to it with deep conviction.

Both of my parents took the time to go visit the kids in the Shriners Hospital, reaching out in tangible ways. My father was part of the Flying Fez and would help transport children to the hospitals. Their memories of the children there are sobering and encompass the ideals of perseverance and grace. This was the greater *why*, the reason behind the reason, that drove them to build better businesses, lives, and communities.

R.E.D. Philosophy

For entrepreneurs, building a better life starts with what I call the MashUp (more on this in the next chapter). If you're only building a career, you won't have the richness and fullness of life experience. But if you're building a life, you'll have a complete circle of relationships with God, your family, and other human beings, and you'll have a strong sense of purpose. When you reflect on how you're just a little piece of this world and universe, you'll still feel full as opposed to insignificant.

So why the R.E.D. philosophy? R.E.D. stands for Ready, Execute, and Deliver. And it's the simplest framework I've found for success.

It's about being READY: Prepared.

My childhood and education was all about getting me ready. It was the foundation for being ready to do what I've done. But really, we can all get ready in different ways—learning, reading, mentorship, and life experiences.

For me, growing up in an entrepreneurial family as the fifth kid was impactful and helped build my foundation. My father was adamant that we all graduated from college. To him, education is the framework for you being teachable.

You know you're ready when you have a grasp of the traits I talked about at the beginning of this chapter—you're bold, confident, and strong, you have a vision, and you're an activator. Now it's time to execute and deliver. It's time to define your win.

EXECUTE: Process.

You're ready . . . now do it. This is the time when your business plan is executed—and executed well. You are actively working through a plan that requires working well with other people, leading with integrity, applying the knowledge with which you came prepared, and building a strong team.

DELIVER: Product.

Hitting the target. Actually obtaining the goal. You will have to execute repeatedly, but delivering is hitting—or exceeding—the goal. It's the win. And it's what this book is all about.

R.E.D. Questions

READY

What is one daily habit you could adopt (like putting on your big deal boots) that would make you feel ready to take on your toughest challenges?

EXECUTE

What is one goal that you absolutely know is worth the effort and then some? What are you doing to move closer to this goal?

DELIVER

Does your goal have a specific finish line? What will the moment look like when you cross that finish line?

READY. EXECUTE. DELIVER.

CHAPTER 2

MashUp and Give

I t's easy; just do it all. Run a business, volunteer, be a good friend, raise a family, support your spouse, and do it all well. If your head is spinning, it's understandable. Mine used to be, too. Here's my suggestion, take a step back—*and a deep breath*—and realize you don't have to do it all. A strategy called MashUp has been a guiding principle in my life and has allowed my entrepreneurial spirit to thrive, but not at the expense of the rest of my life.

MashUp is different from the philosophy of work-life balance due to its perspective that life is not static. Instead, it's a recognition that your life is like an atom with protons and electrons constantly swirling in motion. Life is not a screenshot in time. It's never frozen, so it can never truly be balanced. It's dynamic and constantly shifting according to your season of life. In certain time frames, you may look out of balance. But in reality, it's about getting in sync with your own healthy rhythm and cadence that works best for you. Just like your genes, it's unique to you.

Unlike the philosophy of work-life balance, in which one is constantly under pressure to find the perfect recipe of the right amount of work, the right amount of family, and so on, MashUp promotes the idea that the process is fluid and there is no perfect recipe. It's not about living life one way or the other—it's all of the factors in your life coming together. MashUp is all the elements of you: your relationships, your career, your history, your plans, your home, your activities, and your well-being, all swirling together to build your unique life.

MashUp Makes It Work

MashUp means you make it work. I did exactly that in 2011 when I was leading a high-growth law firm that was involved in a high-stakes, commercial litigation case. Right around the time I had my first baby, our family was displaced because of a flood. Three weeks later, I traveled out of state to complete major-witness depositions.

At night, I was back in my hotel room, planning the baptism of my new baby (an important tradition in my Lutheran faith). While I was gone, my husband had moved our family back into our main home, and I returned to a different house than I had left at the beginning of the week.

To some, this sounds wildly "out of balance." For me, it was a perfect mash-up of faith, family, and work. Not every week is so extreme, but it's a great example of how your life often melts together and it's not about tipping the scale one way or another to make sure everything balances perfectly, but instead embracing the best of each aspect of your life and helping it all work together.

MashUp and Maximize

MashUp fuels business success. It makes you relatable. No one, and I mean no one, can perfectly compartmentalize each aspect of their life, because life flows from one area to another. Your faith, home life, community, and family are all extensions of who you are. Having a good MashUp means you have strong relationships with people. It arms you with the capability to be transparent, authentic, and real. It makes you more relatable as a leader.

I think of the time my husband gave me diamond earrings that I had wanted for years. One day, one of the earrings went missing and we discovered our dog Timo had eaten one of them. It took two weeks of sifting through our little Yorkie's "stuff" before we finally found it. I shipped the earrings off to the jeweler. Guess what? I'm wearing the earrings now. Timo, at my feet and wagging his tail, reminded me to keep it all in perspective. It's the richness and fullness of life that keeps you grounded and humble.

Humility is directly related to vulnerability. If you have a good MashUp, people will see that you are human and you will be a more effective leader. People will simply want to know you more.

A good MashUp also maximizes your time—one of the most precious commodities you possess. When you have a good

MashUp with your time, there is a feeling of freedom and control. Even if you're unsteady in different elements of your life, nothing is going to spin out of control if you have been purposeful with your time.

A good MashUp often bears beautiful fruit. When we experienced the flood in 2011, there was a tremendous outpouring of support and help. We lived on the Missouri River, and I was eight months pregnant when I sent a text message to six friends on Memorial Day weekend. It said the river was rising and we planned to move out that night. I started to go into pre-term labor from the stress.

To my surprise, dozens of people showed up at our house and stayed until 5 a.m., loading our vans. I was moved and inspired to witness the goodness of people in our time of need. A good MashUp will lead you to invest in people, and in turn, invest in life.

The Giving Effect

Giving is easy to do, in small doses here and there, for people you care about or for reasons that might benefit you. It's a difficult, yet greater, thing to allow giving to permeate every corner of your life. In essence, a giver cultivates a consistent "we" over "me" mentality.

I was in first grade when the importance of being a giver first impacted me. I attended school at the time with a boy whom I will refer to as Matt. He lived with a grandparent, wore hand-me-down clothes, and had trouble getting to school on time.

It was tradition in our classroom that you could bring treats on your birthday, and most of us brought popular candy at the time like Skittles and Starburst. When it was Matt's birthday, he excitedly brought us candy. But it was generic, and since it was from Matt, "it had germs." The kids refused to eat it, and he was crushed.

Matt appeared later in my life in a professional capacity. I nominated him to win a prestigious award, and he ended up winning. He and his wife are very successful and have a beautiful family.

But I will never forget how he was treated in school, and I will always regret holding back when I should have done something. Being a giver sometimes has nothing to do with money or material possessions and has everything to do with giving kindness, your attention, your talent, and your support.

Today, it means that I do more than I did back then. I recognize the importance of building others up, and I am purposeful in giving key introductions and compliments. It's simple, and it transforms people.

When you are in the giving moment, you're giving to help someone outside yourself. That, in itself, will change the way you view yourself, your purpose, and your energy throughout the day. Your mission and the momentum that comes along with it will be different if you approach your day fully engaged in giving and not taking.

A giver will sincerely seek ways to help other people and make a difference. At work, givers stay late and go the extra mile. They want to produce more than they take. They have a magnetism that you want to be around. The team is stronger when it is comprised of givers.

I am often encouraged and grateful when I get a thank-you note in the mail. It's one of the fun ways I try to measure how effective I have been in my giving and sharing. When I get notes in the mail, it is an indication that I have made enough of an impact on someone's life that they took the time to physically send me a note.

Maintaining a giving attitude means that you will attract opportunities in ways you could never imagine. It goes back to the idea of investing. When you invest in others, whether it is a stranger or someone you love, it has a ripple effect that will eventually touch you.

A giving mentality will change your spirit and your attitude for the better. You will either be known as a giver or a taker, particularly in business. You can spot the takers. You can see them coming, and you know they are in it for themselves and life is about how everything can benefit them.

The givers make you want what they've got.

Giving Culture

Creating a giving culture will impact your business, your employees, and ultimately your customers. It's a standard that should run through every vein of your company or organization, from the top to the bottom.

It starts with hiring givers over takers. You can tell the difference during the interview. Ask experiential questions: "how would you?" … and fill in the blank. It's not about the answer or accomplishment; it's about their perspective on the situation.

I would ask, "How would you throw a birthday party?" If they answer, "I don't throw birthday parties. My spouse does that," it might be a red flag.

If they make it about the person for whom they're throwing the party—how much their 7-year-old loves Power Rangers or the look on their 90-year-old grandmother's face when she opened the door to the surprise party—it might indicate that they are a giver. In turn, this gives me a window into how they will treat their coworkers and clients.

It's the same with you—treat your employees and co-workers well. Every interaction you have with them impacts your culture and client experiences. Your team will be more engaged if you are a giver. One of the best ways a leader can give is by getting everyone on their team into the perfect role. To do this at my firm, we use StrengthsFinder 2.0, and it absolutely creates an engaged culture and strong team.

Be the Lead Giver

A strong team and organization will be more productive as a whole if everyone is doing their best work rather than operating on the back of one superstar. When you're working on a great team, it's easier, more satisfying, and you get more done faster.

If you hate your coworkers, you're inefficient. You're more likely to give your best if you're encouraged and empowered by people you trust who are also giving their best.

A really awesome team will not tolerate takers. In the medical context, you hear, "This surgeon is amazing, but they have a terrible bedside manner." Or, you hear about an incredibly effective attorney who makes lots of money. But, the team around them will wear out.

This giving culture gives you a sticky team. Maintaining a strong workforce is so hard in today's economy, and you want the best performing team you can get. Having a strong team and getting culture and stickiness is the greatest competitive advantage.

A giving culture attracts and retains clients and customers. You're striving for "wow" experiences for clients. To have a team that can step up and execute a "wow" experience requires a giving culture. And it requires having a finger on the pulse of what impresses your clients. What wows me is different than what wows someone else.

My primary clients oftentimes are CEOs or people in leadership positions. Many of them are older than me and operate in a different social circle. I have to work to figure out their hobbies, interests, and pain points. It means stepping into someone else's shoes to figure out what will wow them in the moment.

Without creating wow experiences, you are a commodity, and people shop on price. But if you can create an experience in which people want to spend their time with you and your organization, and they value that time, they will pay more for it. Then, you won't have to compete just on price.

It develops trust.

In business you will have things go wrong. You will fail and have bad moments. One of the most powerful things you can do to recover is create wow moments.

Part of being a great leader is learning how to create a wow moment out of those tough experiences. If I know we dropped the ball on something, how do I react? If the client thinks they're going to get a letter from us on Tuesday, but they don't get it until Wednesday, I'll call them. Simply owning the mistake can be a wow because it's so rare today.

The next step is being intentional in how you correct an error. I might personally get involved or rally the whole leadership team. The point is to create a major home run out of a bad situation. This is one of the best ways to wow people. As a leader, learn to master a wow turnaround.

This is your opportunity to build trust with your team. They'll be more forthright when they make a mistake, and your client will be more loyal as you build more trust.

If we're moving toward a culture that is not all about ME, it's best to start small. Reflect on your intentions in all facets of your life—do you give more than you take? If not, make a commitment to small changes. Challenge yourself to purposely give one compliment per day, whether it's to the grocery store checker or to your child's teacher.

Don't be afraid to measure it and keep yourself accountable. You know how I do it? I track how many thank-you notes I receive. It's not a shrine to myself! Rather, it's a great feedback loop to quantify the impact I'm having. If nothing else, it's a reminder that you have made a difference in the life of someone else—and sometimes in the best ways. Some of my favorite thank-you notes were for an introduction, an experience, or an opportunity. Those are the things money can't easily buy.

R.E.D. Questions

READY

Are you ready to let go of the idea that each aspect of your life will fit into a perfect little box, neatly wrapped up with a bow on it? Are you ready to let go of this concept that you're in control?

EXECUTE

Are you willing to give more than you take? How will you measure this?

DELIVER

Who will hold you accountable for following through on your new actions?

PART TWO

EXECUTE

READY. EXECUTE. DELIVER.

CHAPTER 3

R.E.D. Mentality

Are you sold out, invested, not going back? If going "all in" isn't your mindset, I promise you have lost a major competitive advantage. Why? Imagine two boxers stepping into the ring. The first has adrenaline surging through his body. The second is nervous and timid. Who will win? Obviously, the first boxer will because he is *all in*. Even if they've trained equally hard, it's the mindset in the moment that will make all the difference. In the same way, the entrepreneurs who train the proper muscles *and* show up with a mind that's *all in* are the ones who win big.

Before you think this is too dramatic, I wear an Apple watch with a heart rate monitor, and it's telling of the days when I am in the ring, when I'm going to battle for my career. It's often during a major mediation or court day, when my skills, time, talent, and preparation all converge. I can see the victory clearly—and my heart rate is legitimately higher.

It's your game time. Get ready and step into the ring, knowing that much of your battle is mental. You're a hustler, and that's the competitive edge. If your competitor isn't completely invested the way you are, even if they have more resources, you're going to beat them. When David faced Goliath, he wasn't thrown off by the incredible size of the giant standing before him. David was mentally prepared for battle, used his resources (a rock and a slingshot) with purpose, and took down his opponent.

What commitment do you have to succeed, and can you recognize when you're not all in? I think of when we opened an office in Fargo, North Dakota. I saw an opportunity and was attracted to the possibilities of a junior attorney in a small office complex. But, I'll be honest: I wasn't 100 percent sold. That office failed within nine months.

Flip the coin. When I opened an office in Omaha, Nebraska, I could feel it in my bones—I was all in. I took greater risks, including partnering with one of the most successful attorneys in the state. I invested more time. I'm there two days a week. I hired 20 people within a year and a half.

In North Dakota, I dipped my toe in the water. If it failed, it wouldn't hurt too much. But that is a problematic mindset, because whether you are aware of it or not, you hold back. When there is much to lose, your foot is on the pedal and you're pushing hard for a greater outcome.

I'm one hundred percent committed in Omaha—my reputation is on the line. Failure is not an option because I took great risks and I've seen great dividends because of it. What are you holding back from going all in on? If you're not sold on an idea, it's OK. Are you hungry enough to go back to the drawing board if needed? Find the right idea and go out on the limb. Be so invested that there is no Plan B. Failure is not an option.

Executing

You stand on the cusp of making one of the biggest career decisions of your life, and one of the pivotal questions that needs to be asked and answered is, "Is it worth it?" The time, the money, the sacrifice. If the answer is YES, how do you know if you are prepared?

Research

Have you armed yourself with the very best tools and resources? How well do you know your craft, the market, your customers, and your competitors? Do your research, thoroughly and consistently. Your level of competency directly relates to the amount of research you do. A small amount of research will only put you on par with your competitors. When your knowledge simply matches theirs, you haven't gained the upper hand. Up your game, research more, and you will know more than your competitor. It will give you a competitive advantage, but it still doesn't make you an expert.

So, I encourage you to do so much research that you become a master in your area of expertise. The knowledge you acquire will become innate. Have you ever driven home, pulled into your driveway, and wondered how you got there? Or, have you ever taken a dance class and by the end, you didn't even have to think about the moves? It's called muscle memory, and it will serve you well as an entrepreneur.

Becoming a master is right on track with what we talked about when we described going "all in." Your research to start a business is in-depth and uncovers every corner of the unknown. Your plan is detailed and includes the amount of capital you will need, your staff make-up, and a look at what other people have done in similar circumstances.

Plant Some Seeds

A solid plan starts with planting seeds. It could be as simple as having coffee with a friend, years before you move forward with your idea, to simply plant the seed that could someday lead to you asking them to become part of your staff or invest in your business.

It could be a phone call, a conversation, an envelope of cash you keep that could be your first investment—all of it just smooths the road for when you are ready for your dream to unfold. Seed planting might actually start years or months ahead. I remember updating my managing partner on how the firm was going, long before we ever agreed to work together. Sometimes all you need to do is drop those small signs and know that they could bear fruit later.

Doors of opportunity open more quickly and wider when you have planted seeds. You're not starting from scratch, and since you've prepared by planting seeds, you are ready to make a solid plan.

Planting seeds is about one thing—foresight. For my Omaha office, I had a list of people whom I wanted to be part of my team. I didn't reveal to those people they were on the list, but I was doing the behind-the-scenes work to prepare for the day when I would ask. It's thoughtful. It's smart. It's strategic.

Once you've planted seeds, you're ready and you have the resources to create your master plan.

Know Your Outcome

Speaking of strategic, your next step is to know your outcome. What exactly does a win look like to you? You should be able to define it and write it down. It could be resources, revenue, building the perfect team, winning a case. Goals are specific to you and can be flexible for the season you are in. At first, a win might involve influencing public opinion. A loss might actually be building for the future, laying the groundwork for a future win.

Or, maybe you're strategically doing what you're doing for a win or loss simply to distract your competitor. I want to be clear about this. All of your hard work, go-get-it attitude, seed planting, and executing will be for naught if you don't play fairly. I'm all about crushing the competition, but doing it the right way. Make sure that you are within every moral, legal, and ethical boundary, and the reputation you need to build will start to build itself on its way. We all know that word travels fast, and nothing travels faster than information that someone is not playing by the rules. When in doubt, go the extra mile to do the right thing. Don't even let there be an appearance of gray. Play above the boards. It's a code of conduct that will pay great dividends someday.

Back to executing. When I have set my goals and decided what a win will look like, I keep it in front of me. Literally. I print out my goals, laminate them, and set them somewhere that I have to see them frequently. When I was in law school, I taped my goals to the mirror in my apartment.

To this day, I keep my current goals in my purse. I can't avoid it. It's a tangible reminder of where I want to be. It's written with my hand, so it's personal. The accountability keeps me hungry and humble. The gap between where I am and where I want to be keeps me humble.

Make Room

Make sure you have the capacity to be all in. No one will be more committed than you. You can hire amazing talent and a great team around you. You can even hire expert consultants, but you need to know there will be some loneliness. But if you are going to make it happen, it all comes back to you. Success or failure rides on your shoulders.

You've got to make room to be all in. Make room within that MashUp we talked about. My family knows I'm gone two days a week, but they know that and support me. I've freed up financial capital to make it happen, and we create room in the schedule to make it possible. And when I'm gone from the office, my team knows they'll have to cover things that I would normally do. You have to make changes and let go of the way things were in order to shift, and that means having a strong team. It also means having the right team.

The *Right* Team

Just because you have one team to accomplish one particular goal doesn't mean it's the same team for the next one. A strong football team cannot be a strong swim team. Sometimes, the team who got you to where you are today isn't the team that will get you to where you're going next. Different goals require a different team. Certain people might be on your team for one project, but it might be a different mix of people for the next. Teams evolve and seasons change, and just like in sports, players get traded every season. Heck, even coaches change sometimes. So build the team that will get the win for the game you're playing today.

Collecting Wins

Victories come in all sizes. You might have to stage small wins to gain momentum as you move toward your big goal. There are times when I intentionally create an opportunity to encourage an employee. I might assign smaller tasks to help them find success. If you can give people a taste of the win, you build their confidence and morale.

At my office, if I anticipate falling short on a goal, I'll create other ways for us to have smaller wins to boost the momentum. Maybe we landed three clients. Maybe we increased our client retention rate from the year before. With momentum, we can then hit the overarching goal.

It's important to have metrics that are measurable and attainable. You have to break down goals into bite sizes, because nobody else will do that for you. Hitting smaller goals also increases belief. The process of creating small wins will remove all doubt on why you are the leader. This reinforces your confidence in attaining the bigger goal, and in where you're going.

Not everyone will cheer you on as you collect wins. Your circle will support you, but your success will draw haters. People will be jealous and talk you down. The bigger the wins, the more people want a piece of you. It can create confusion—who is really on your team? And if someone wants to be part of your team, is it genuine or do they just want to take a part of what you have earned?

Going All In

In the end, one of the greatest benefits of going all in (and winning) is that you are giving. You're planting seeds for future opportunities. Sometimes you don't even know why you're giving or investing, but you can trust that it will come back to you someday. The seeds you've planted before may come to fruition in a future plan in a way you never imagined. Continually planting seeds by giving, taking action, and being an activator needs to become a way of life and work. It will lead to more abundance than you ever thought possible by making future plans flourish.

R.E.D. Questions

READY

Is your goal worth it? Is your goal worth going all in?

EXECUTE

Is it worth it for you to do whatever it takes? Have you written down your goal? Have you shared it with other people? Have you taken action to commit your resources?

DELIVER

Have you built momentum by setting up small wins?

READY. EXECUTE. DELIVER.

CHAPTER 4

R.E.D. Deals

A *R.E.D. deal is a Big Deal.*

R.E.D. deals are rare, game-changing, and can light the kind of fire under your business that you've only dreamt about. They are also dangerous. The strategies I've honed over the years will prepare you, show you how to make them happen, and execute with finesse.

I probably don't have to tell you how to recognize a Big Deal—you'll feel it in your gut. It could be landing the client who will keep your doors open for the next decade. It could be an acquisition, selling the business, or leveraging every resource you have to win during litigation.

It's intense, and your company will not be the same after the deal happens. If you win, it's amazing. If you lose, it's terrible. The risk is incredibly high, because remember, you're all in.

R.E.D. deals manifest themselves when you have a desire for them to show up and you have laid the foundation and framework for success. You're ready. Sometimes, a R.E.D. deal is actually walking away from or breaking ties with a job or business partner.

It was a pivotal moment in my career when I left my partnership at a very successful law firm.

You know it's a R.E.D. moment when the future is in your hands, you're standing at a fork in the road, and the weight of the decision is heavy. It's powerful, exhilarating, and scary, all at the same time. Some people grow addicted to the adrenaline of these deals.

Timing a R.E.D. deal is everything. Move too slowly, and it's gone. Move too quickly, and you'll kill it. Mastering the cadence of a R.E.D. deal is imperative. This is where your research, your entrepreneurial drive, and your nerves of steel all come together to help you navigate the timing of the deal.

Waiting too long risks losing the momentum and watching the deal fizzle out. If you rush too quickly, people can get cold feet and back out. If it's simply the wrong timing, market forces could snuff it out. The right pace is key. Keep the cadence.

Know when you're out of your league, or if you can play ball. Experience matters in life-changing deals. The first time you do a major deal, you're playing with fire, and it's not a place for amateurs. Allow for only one driver, who sets the pace, tone, and momentum.

This driver lays out the strategy, oversees the execution, and acts as the battle warrior who will get you to the other side. You trust them. In a project with multiple phases, there may be multiple leaders, but there needs to be one clear point person on your side.

For a deal that is more complex, with more players and parties, it's even more important to have a clear leader. Once the phase is done, they pass off the baton.

R.E.D. deals draw heat. This is also the time to remember that not everyone plays nice. Don't be surprised if someone from your past decides to unearth a few of your skeletons. If you're making R.E.D. deals, politics plays a part. There's a reason I'm a registered lobbyist. It doesn't have to haunt you, but be proactive by creating a comprehensive political and public relations plan in advance.

At the Table

Be aware that different parties come to the table, and there are a handful of characters who can get a R.E.D. deal off track if you don't spot them ahead of time and adjust accordingly.

- **The Projector:** They are the smartest people in the room and puff themselves up to feel worthy. They are insecure and their goal is to intimidate.
- **The Pretender:** They have hidden intentions. To the outer world, they pretend their intentions are pure. They can fool you if you don't realize their true motivations.
- **The Confused:** They are emotionally confused. These are the type of people paralyzed by indecisiveness who need some hand-holding. R.E.D. deals often change the life of the individuals involved, and when the stakes are that high, this type of person will lose their way in emotions and fear.

- **The Hesitator:** This person drags their feet and throws off the cadence. They've done the work, but can't sign on the dotted line. They have a million excuses on why they're hesitating. At the end of the day, they just can't follow through.
- **The Whisperer:** There is one more person to be on the lookout for, and that's The Whisperer. This person is a tangential player in the game—a spouse, a mentor, a business coach, or anyone who has the ear of the decision makers. This person might even be the matriarch of the family who is actually making the business decisions. Regardless, The Whisperer plays an integral part in a R.E.D. deal—though sometimes behind-the-scenes.

The makeup of your team will also make a big difference in the outcome. You want experience, talent, and movers and shakers. You want the best, and they might look like this:

- **The Motivated:** This person has the motivation to make the deal successful. They are invested and they are ready to execute. They deliver.
- **The Linchpin:** They will benefit the most after the deal closes. They have the experience, talent, and fire-hardened ability. They are professionals who have been trained and educated and, most importantly, have sealed deals before. They could be a trial lawyer, a commericial realtor, or an investment banker.

There's no need to be overwhelmed by who's who. The lines often blur between the vested and the deal killers. Just keep the goal in mind and keep your team close.

Ready

Imagine you're in court with the opponent's key witness on the stand. You show the witness Exhibit A, and the witness denies ever seeing the document. You have the key to the case riding on whether this witness sent this email. This is the exhibit that shows intent and proves the case. Movies love this moment. The drama is real.

Any trial lawyer worth their weight would be prepared, deposition in hand, able to impeach the witness and discredit their testimony, working with mastery. Experienced trial lawyers move swiftly on their feet and feed off opportunities to cross-examine the other side.

It's the same with R.E.D. deals. If you're all in, it means you have invested, sacrificed, and worked to the bone to get to this point—the point in which you stand on the cusp of a deal that could change your business and your life.

Please, don't get to the finish and realize you can't cross because you didn't prepare. How do you know if you're prepared? Cross-check these elements to make sure you're on the right track.

Element #1

Have your head in the game. Remember our key players who could threaten the life of the deal? You're not one of those, so be a vested party, be present, be a person of integrity. Do whatever you need to be emotionally and mentally prepared. Lean on your faith, take a vacation, take a walk, confide in your attorney, and get some rest. If your head is not in the game, you're not going to be able to fully execute.

Element #2

Clean up those skeletons. Talk them through with your trusted advisor. Be honest. Yes, it can be emotional. It can be painful. You're vulnerable. But there conversations are crucial, and you will gain nothing by avoiding them. It could be that you have a former business partner who is now a competitor. Or, you have a former spouse that you are up against. Don't ignore the emotional baggage. Keep your eye on the prize, be a person of integrity and be prepared for how you might feel by having conversations with someone with whom you have a history.

Element #3

Know what you want. Sometimes the hardest part is figuring out what kind of outcome you want. Ask yourself what a win in this deal looks like. If you want to acquire a company, why? If it's because you can sell more, why does that matter? Your answer might be because you want to do A, B, C, and D. Then your goal isn't to simply acquire the company, it's to do A, B, C, and D. When you understand the ultimate goals, there are things you can negotiate to get what you want. There are other roads you can take. When obstacles come up, and you know what you want, you can maneuver through those obstacles.

Execute

When a big deal comes along, you will execute with excellence, capitalize on the opportunity, and not be slowed down.

The first step to doing that is assembling your success team. For this particular deal, your team may be different than the previous deal. You need to have the right players at the table to support you and get you where you need to go. You should know these players before you actually need them.

For example, if you own a business you plan to sell five to seven years down the road, anticipate the type of team you would like in advance. Time is wasted if you're scrambling to meet people, attempting to build relationships and synergy at the last minute.

Secondly, identify your driver. You may be the driver, but you also might not be. Sometimes you have to put your faith and trust in another person and let go of the steering wheel.

True wisdom is admitting when you're out of your league. Check your ego at the door and find the best person to lead. Strong leaders know when they need help.

Finally, have a plan but be flexible. Pivot when you hit an unmovable roadblock. You must be nimble and able to take some punches. Don't be so set in your ways that you can't learn and adjust as you move through the process. There are multiple paths to a destination, and if you are so married to your plan and unable to change, you could lose out.

Deliver

If you're going to win big deals with excellence, you must consistently compete, strategize, and negotiate.

If you're not a fierce competitor, you're not up for the challenge. We call ourselves sharks, one of the fiercest predators on the planet. It's written into the DNA of a shark—the bite, the power, prominence, and wherewithal. You're willing to stack up everything you've got to win this big deal, because you're competing to win. It doesn't mean you're cruel or rude. Being respectful and competitive are not mutually exclusive. You can be both. Winners love to compete.

You must be strategic. Big deals require perspective. See obstacles approaching and anticipate how you will react. You can operate well down in the trees and then take a step back and view the forest. The ability to maintain perspective gives you an advantage.

Creating a strategy beyond tactics is smart. For example, when I do a big deal, I come up with themes. Great trial lawyers have themes, for example, to help your story resonate with the jury. Themes lay out your presentation in a way that is convincing and believable. During a big deal, it's a reminder of why you're in the deal.

And there is no greater secret tool than being a great negotiator. In the same way you lay out your themes, mark small negotiation points. These are the small battles to win along the way to winning the war. There's some give and take in the smaller points, but be the shark on the big ones. Knowing which is which takes intuition, and we'll talk more about that soon.

R.E.D. Questions

READY

Are you ready for the change? Are you embracing what's on the other side of this deal?

EXECUTE

Have you laid the foundation? Do you have the right plan and success team to get you through the deal? Do you have the right resources to execute?

DELIVER

Are you a strategic competitor? Is it worth it to compete in this arena for the deal?

READY. EXECUTE. DELIVER.

CHAPTER 5

R.E.D. Negotiation

"Winning isn't everything." It's an important adage we pass along to our children, but here, this is about much more than sports or childhood games. You're all in, which means *it is* important to win, the right way. Use these key strategies for winning important negotiations, and, in the process, get better deals for your company.

I've been through thousands of negotiations, and I can say without flinching that shark negotiations are not for the faint of heart. You have to ask yourself, is this worth the fight? Am I willing to get bloody? You must count the cost, decide whether it is worth it, and move.

If it is worth it, be confident that there are multiple ways to walk into the negotiating room in control and leave in control: Be firm on your non-negotiables, know your competitors and their pain points, and be tenacious.

Recognize that there are no take-backs. Once it's on the table, you can't get it back.

There is room for give, at the right time. Give when it doesn't matter to you.

Most of all, demonstrate that you are engaged. You can be firm, yet malleable enough to keep things moving forward. Decide what is worth fighting for, and take your stand on those items.

Great negotiators know how to properly scale. There's no need to overdo it when it's something small. Don't go in with guns blazing when there is no real threat. Save the guns though; you'll need them for later.

The Negotiation Mentality

Your head should be in the game well before the game. How you think and believe, before you even enter the negotiation, will overshadow your every move.

When I enter a negotiating room, I come with three bullets, and I shoot to kill. My bullets are my three most powerful weapons in each case—pieces of information that can take down the other side. They differ from case to case, and they could have been uncovered during one of my most effective tools, coming to the negotiating table over-prepared.

When I enter negotiations, I am so prepared, it catches the other side off-guard. We might be at a pre-trial conference and I have already completed a mock jury trial. An expert report is not due for another nine months and I slide it across the table. I am confident and calm because I am so far ahead of the game. I have a major advantage.

Your confident mentality sometimes stems from small things: body language, setting the atmosphere with certain food, the location of your meeting space, what color you wear (red for power, of course), or communicating in other non-verbal ways that remind your opponent you are to be taken seriously.

All of these tactics are scalable depending on the size of the deal. If you're negotiating for your life, everything is worth it. If you're negotiating for $100, I wouldn't spend 10 seconds on it.

Remember that every move is carving out your reputation. You are striving to win, in a way that commands respect from opponents. You understand, and embrace, the idea that there will be a winner and a loser. You might be the reason for the other person's loss because you're a good negotiator. That is business. That is life. If you're not OK with that, you shouldn't negotiate R.E.D. deals.

It goes back to self-awareness and recognizing if you're not the right fit. If it's out of your league, be honest. You don't have to be the negotiator; you just want to be the winner. If you're not the best person to walk into that room, delegate to the person who is.

Be prepared to discern this in every area of negotiating. Are you in the varsity league to negotiate a labor agreement with the unions? Just because you're a skilled negotiator in one area doesn't mean you're great in another. Negotiating deals is not universal. You might be a great negotiator buying a car, but negotiating a collective bargaining agreement is not in your wheelhouse.

You have put in the time to practice negotiating, and now it's the real thing. If you aren't confident or get in over your head, reach out to your trusted inner circle and get out of your own way.

You must make each of these decisions with the confidence of a pro. If you have self-doubt, you've crippled your ability to win. You'll never win if you don't think you can. I'll reassign people from my team if they don't think we can win. If you enter any journey with a mindset that you will fail—guess what? You will. Your mindset is everything.

You also possess the power of silence. Be comfortable with it. The power of listening is underestimated. The more you run your mouth, the more your words become diluted and lack power. Silence is a way to not only gain a better perspective of the people around you, but also to increase the effectiveness of what does come out of your mouth. I like to say what I'm going to say and then be silent. Practice this. It's as difficult as it is important.

Negotiating to Win

So what exactly is at the heart of winning negotiations? To be clear, I define a win as hitting your predetermined goal. Goals can shift during the process, but you can't retroactively call something a win. If you did, it's spinning. It's public relations. You didn't really win.

Non-Negotiables

I mentioned the keys to winning a negotiation earlier. Let's take a closer look at them now. The first is to know your non-negotiables. If you know these upfront, you can drive the conversation. It simply helps you maneuver through the negotiation because your non-negotiables are the sacred items you can't, won't, give up. Not everyone needs to know what they are. It can be an advantage to have them hidden. If that's the case, you still need to mean what you say. If you are willing to budge, even a tiny bit, it's negotiable.

Is something truly a non-negotiable? Put it to the test. Ask some hypothetical questions. For example, you have Celiac Disease and you are on a strict gluten-free diet. You're at your grandparents' 50th anniversary party and your great aunt made your favorite family dessert that you can only get from her and this is the last time you'll see her. Are you willing to eat it or not? If you are, it's a negotiable.

These are about testing absolutes, and the number of non-negotiables frequently depends on the size of the deal. If you're selling the company, the other side will probably want the executive team to stay intact and sign non-compete agreements. I can test that by mentioning the possibility of pulling another star employee from another company instead. If you're really creative, you can take a non-negotiable and make it negotiable.

Pain Points

The second key is to know your competitor's pain points, as well as their sweet spots. Remember the old adage that advised keeping your friends close, but your enemies closer? Apply that here. You know their pain points and sweet spots by doing your homework, research, observation, and spending time with them.

In the legal world, we hire local counsel when we venture into foreign states. You want to know patterns and preferences and favorites that are not obvious. Do your due diligence to find out how they operate and indentify their strengths and weaknesses.

When people win, it's because they have been creative in this work. There is no template for which questions to ask. They do the hard work to find the information and nuances of their competitor that will strengthen their own hand during negotiations.

Tenacity

The next key is to be tenacious. This is a trait that can be learned and taught through mentorship. You're riding that line between assertive and aggressive. Tenacity will put you in the trenches, right where you should be. I think about a time early in my career when I was working on a big case with a senior partner. We didn't know enough about the opposing side. He sent me to go stake out the opposing side's operation, from a public road. We learned valuable information through that process.

In law school, I worked on a case in a legal clinic and helped represent a woman who was denied disability benefits. We didn't have the money to hire health experts, so my law professor coached me to chase down busy doctors in hospital parking lots to obtain the expert opinion reports. It worked.

Another time we had a court order to do a site visit. Oddly, the garbage truck showed up to take the garbage on a Tuesday when the city normally takes it on a Thursday. We called the judge on the spot to expand the order to seize the garbage.

In college, I applied for scholarships to help with the cost; those dozens of scholarships helped in a big way. But for every one I received, I received more than one rejection. Then I studied for the law school admissions test to receive a full academic scholarship.

Tenacity can be taught. It's a boldness to ask questions, find experts, think on your feet, learn to be rejected, and do research that will bolster your side or simply throw your competition off kilter. Being tenacious matters, every time. Learn to be rejected.

No Take-Backs

Another key in winning negotiations is recognizing that there are no take-backs. Whatever you offer today, it's out there for good. You have shown your hand, and unless there's a shift in paradigm, there's no going back.

There are rare times when things change, big time. For example, one of you has changed negotiators. Someone filed bankruptcy, fired the CEO, changed law firms, someone has died, or a court ruling is announced. In any such case, you can go back to square one on your offer.

Another key strategy to winning is knowing when to give in, which requires you to stay engaged through the entire process.

If you are not willing to give on some of the negotiables, people will shut down. You are continually making quick judgments on what to leverage, and at exactly the right time. You want to give on the right things when it benefits your client the most.

All the while, you're cognizant that you're dealing with humans and a little grace goes a long way toward protecting your reputation. Someone has had a family vacation scheduled for months and needs a schedule change. If you're willing to give a little, it demonstrates wisdom and will bear fruit in the long run. Don't get stuck on trivial things that could jeopardize your hard work in the long run.

R.E.D. Questions

READY

Have you calculated the cost?

EXECUTE

Have you gotten creative and truly identified the non-negotiables? What are you willing to do?

DELIVER

How will you deliver the win that you've set your mind on?

READY. EXECUTE. DELIVER.

CHAPTER 6

R.E.D. Strategy

If you strip away all the hoopla, the game of basketball is pretty basic. Two teams, five players, one ball, dribble the ball to the hoop and make it into the basket. When you're watching the Final Four, the participants make it look easy. But we all know it isn't that simple. Thousands of coaches and players have strategized plays for the sport since 1891. Strategy within your organization is very much the same. It's how you're playing the game, and how you can do it at a level that will help you find success. Operating with a sound strategy will give your organization credibility, better results, and help you build a legacy in your career, community, and corner of the market.

Good strategy is novel and unique. We've been in the top 100 fastest-growing law firms in the United States. People want to know the secret. We have a strategic plan, and we execute it. When you experience wins borne directly from your strategies, it builds momentum and confidence that will help you scale and grow. Doubters become believers, and that's a major win.

Having a sound strategy will give you confidence as a leader. If it's a good strategy, you'll be energized and confident. You're bound to win. If you feel doubt and fear, it's a red flag indicating you need a better strategy.

An organization or company with a weak strategy or no strategy is exactly that, weak, and will be overcome by competition with a winning strategy. Don't be afraid to reevaluate your strategy. David was very purposeful in the stones he handpicked to take down Goliath. Choose your stones carefully. If you don't have a strategy, go find some stones.

Keep it a Secret

Protect what you do well by not oversharing. Keeping your strategy under wraps is an undervalued competitive advantage. Simply execute and don't worry about external people knowing how you do what you do so well. As long as you are a private enterprise, you have the right to have private plans.

There's power in having a secret strategy. It bonds people together and creates a team atmosphere. Your team will feel like it's on the inside, because they are. After you win, you can announce it to the world.

You win, but you keep playing like there's no score on the scoreboard. Continue working as though you are still the underdog, even if you're not. Even as you grow, stay scrappy, alert, and agile. Don't get comfortable. Companies who continue to perform as though they have something to prove are more likely to find long-term success.

Strengthen Your Strategy

Reflect on how you establish and process strategy with these questions: Do I create an edge? Do I make plans on how we're going to win? Is this my strength and talent? Do I employ creative ideas? Have I ever written down strategies?

If you have nothing in writing, it's a problem. If strategy is not your strength, put people on your team who do it well.

Strategy is about leveraging your resources to find success in the future. Do you have a 1-year strategic plan for how you're going to win? A 5-year strategic plan? What about 10? If you don't have one, get one.

Honestly, it's rare for a business to have a current written strategy and written goals. That's why it's a competitive advantage.

To get there, sometimes you need to get out. Stepping outside of your environment can help clear your mind and give you a fresh take on your business or organization. Go on vacation. Book some beach time and bring along a notebook. You'll be amazed at what becomes clear when you're out of the daily stresses. I schedule a focus day each quarter. It's my think-tank time, and I count on it to force me out of the daily grind.

Key conversations can provide the same kind of perspective as a great day at the beach. Sometimes we get so far down the rabbit hole, we can't remember why we started what we started. A quality conversation with people in a different industry can give you great ideas on new and exciting strategies. How can you modify the great things they are doing to fit your industry? For example, I take a lot of ideas for our law firm from the financial services industry and deploy them in the legal industry.

Sometimes, the conversations are even more insightful when they are with other leaders within your industry. I love national conferences for this very reason. You can leave your competitive landscape to meet peers who are looking for the same thing you are—encouragement, ideas, market updates, and synergy. I walk away from every national conference with connections, and more importantly, new ideas for how to improve my strategy. We have a saying called "R&D," meaning rip off and duplicate. It doesn't mean you run around copying everybody, but you don't have to be completely original in your strategies. They just need to be contextualized and tailored to your specific business. The bottom line is that you can, and should, learn from your peers.

Is it Worth It?

I have a barometer of sorts that we use to measure our investments, a laminated and framed document consisting of our Mission-

Vision-Values statement. It's a reminder of what is "worth it" as we decide how to use our time, talent, and treasure. Certain strategies will cost more, and having the mission before us in black and white sets the foundation and backbone for how we determine strategies.

Mission: Worth it

You want to be everything to everyone. The answer "yes" can slip out of your mouth too often, too quickly. Your mission will keep you in check and keep you from taking on too much. If it doesn't directly support the mission, it's out. The mission helps you identify your strategies and determine whether or not they're the right ones.

When you work this out practically, your mission becomes the litmus test for every decision. Do we take on a new client? Is it worth it?

Do we hire this new person at this compensation package? Is it worth it?

Do we go in to work every day? Is it worth it?

And when your client gets your bill, it better be worth it.

Vision: To be the Law Firm of Choice in the Midwest

You know the vision is right when it inspires you. You have to know *where* you're going so can you take the appropriate steps to get there. Your vision is the spotlight to guide the way.

The scope of a vision is tricky. It needs to be broad enough to allow for some wiggle room, yet defined in a way that's clear. Your strategy answers the question of *how* are we going to get there, but vision really addresses the question of *where* we are going.

Your vision inspires your team daily. It drives them to continue pushing on to the next stepping stone, because they have an idea of where this is all headed. If your vision doesn't inspire people, they're not going to stay. That's OK. Let them go.

Values: The What

You set the bar, from dress code to the code of conduct. Set the expectations within your organization and take them seriously. These expectations establish our values. Each team member has to embody our values to advance. That can be hard.

One of our Goosmann values, for example, is positivity. It's OK if you're not off-the-charts enthusiastic, but we expect a consistent effort to look at the bright side and find a way to win. It's about more than just a cheery disposition. It's about our overall values, including quality, growth, productivity, and culture. Each of those aspects is unique to us.

Make sure that your values align with your organization and the team you have assembled. For example, if you struggle with growth and change, our law firm would not be a good fit for you. A leader's values will permeate every area of your organization.

Beliefs: The How

Beliefs will be the lens through which you see all things in your business or organization. At our law firm, we have a giving mindset, we believe that passion fuels success, we believe in setting high goals, and we believe the team is everything.

If you're not operating on a set of beliefs, both internally and externally, you will get off course. The beliefs behind the organization are the compass. Team members who don't agree with our beliefs will not last long at our firm. They simply can't thrive if they haven't bought in to the belief system.

We have a saying that when you sign on with us, you're given a pair of Goosmann goggles. If you're on the team, you adopt our beliefs and it is the perspective through which you view our work. If you can't see clearly, we are not the right fit.

Results

Execution on your strategy creates results. Results may come in immediately, and others will trickle in over time. The immediate impact of initial results will give you clarity, personal power, momentum, and focus moving forward. Positive results that come immediately will empower you to continue. You're a force because you've embraced your strategy, and that feels good.

Results can be quantified. What was the 90-day impact on your organization? Tracking consistently gives you momentum. Every Monday, we do a power hour with our leadership team. We track our critical sprint initiatives. We are either on or off track after the quarter. It's about focus, drive, and accountability.

What does your organization look like after a year? It better look like success. People love winning, and they want to be on the winning team. When you create strategies for goals and execute on them, you can win.

And finally, what does your organization look like in the long term? People want what you have and don't know how to get there. You collect accolades and accomplishments. People look up to you, marveling at how you implemented your strategy in a way that led you to success.

R.E.D. Questions

READY

What's your goal? How are you going to get there? Have you written down your goal? Have you verbally committed to that goal in your organization? Have you set aside the time to think?

EXECUTE

Have you budgeted behind the strategy? Have you put the right people in place? Are you acting as though you already are where you want to be? Are your strategies big enough to accomplish your goals?

DELIVER

Have you encouraged your team to be strategic as well? Is your strategy so big that it's cascading through your organization?

READY. EXECUTE. DELIVER.

CHAPTER 7

R.E.D. Stress

When you're doing big R.E.D. deals, you accept the responsibility that these are game changers for the client, the company, your team, and you personally, and the ramifications or outcomes lie in your hands. Feel the pressure yet? How do you develop the mentality and strategy to perform at a high level when the stress, and sometimes risk, is just as high?

What you're doing is not a game. If the company goes under, it affects real people. It changes lives. Every R.E.D. deal is a stressful deal, no matter the dollar amount. You might be handling a deal worth $100,000 and it affects a small business, or it could be like an Erin Brockovich deal and touch the lives of every family in the case. The stress can paralyze you, or it can be harnessed for some good. Let's see how.

Peak Performance

The diamond. It's rare, expensive, and one of the most sought-after gems on every continent since its discovery in India in 4th Century B.C. The diamond is the hardest known material in the world, having formed more than 100 miles below the earth's surface. It is only in temperatures greater than 2,000 degrees Fahrenheit and under more than 725,000 pounds-per-square-inch that natural graphite is transformed into a diamond.

If you are doing R.E.D. deals, you have to be the diamond— the kind of rock that can withstand the heat and the intense pressure to be compressed into the very best version of yourself. Stress can do just that. It can crush us, or it can push us to our peak performance.

Reaching your peak performance is not without a keen sense of perspective and balance. You don't want stress to hinder your ability to perform at your highest levels. You want stress, in rea- sonable amounts, to serve as a motivating factor to do better, help you establish boundaries, tune up your brain and improve your performance.

In my years as an attorney, I've seen stress impact people in different ways. I have witnessed the way it can force you to carve out the right priorities, whittle away at your weaknesses, and push you to take one more step than you thought you could. I have witnessed people under consistent, incredible pressure manage it in a way that the weight of the stress didn't crush them, but instead helped them become stronger.

Stress is like anything else: If it's not managed, it will cripple your performance. You can't be at your peak performance if you are struggling with stress and hindered by the anxiety it introduces. According to the Centers for Disease Control, stress can take an incredible toll on the body, including loss of appetite, nightmares, headaches, sleep problems, back pains, stomach aches, and a lack of concentration, among other things.

I have also seen people develop stress behaviors like stress ticks, their face and neck getting flushed and red, talking too fast, sighing deeply, pacing, running their hands through their hair, and biting their fingernails.

As an attorney, I've also seen it impact people in the long-term in three major ways: people burn out, quit, or get in trouble. They turn to negative coping mechanisms like alcohol or gambling. Some of the above physical and mental symptoms were a precursor to the longer-term effects of stress that were left unchecked.

I don't say all this to scare you. I offer it as a sober reminder. Stress is real for many people, and if you are doing R.E.D. deals, it's part of life. You are operating in a world of stress, and you better figure out healthy ways to manage it.

If you don't love what you're doing, the stress isn't worth it. It is physically and mentally exhausting, and it will eat you up if you don't have the passion or the drive for what you are doing.

If it's not worth it, you'll opt out or be forced out. Survival of the fittest applies in business.

But, when you love it, the work feeds your soul. Your adrenaline kicks in with each new assignment or challenge. You view stress as merely a hurdle to get over, not a roadblock. You crave the challenge. You almost become addicted.

As a leader, are you going to place more responsibilities into the hands of the person who has the clear symptoms of stress? Or do you want to work with the person who feeds off of stress?

Good leadership will delegate to the right people according to each team member's strengths, weaknesses, experiences, and stress management skills. It's about putting people in the right place at the right time, with the capacity to tackle the job. As the stakes go higher, so must the capability of the team members.

I have a healthy affinity for stress in my job. Every R.E.D. deal is stressful by nature because it is a game changer for you, your employees, the client, and the community. It's never lost on me that the outcome of what I am leading will affect real people.

The larger the dollar amount, the greater the pressure. It once was a million-dollar deal, and now it might be a billion-dollar deal. The outcome of a R.E.D. deal with such dollar amounts will have a ripple effect for years. That is powerful, and I feel the weight of it on my shoulders.

It's worth it. Sometimes it's not even about money, but about doing the right thing. Sometimes you're on the side of good and if you win, it will truly make a difference in the world. It's stressful when the stakes are that high, because you are drawn to that win like a magnet.

High Stakes, High Performance

How you manage stress, and help those around you manage stress, will affect the outcome of everyone's work at your organization. Management starts with knowing exactly how you react to stress.

Know yourself and your trigger points. When is your judgment clouded? What are your indicators of when you need to seek help? Check your ego at the door and get outside help if you are overwhelmed.

I think of when it came time to write the company bylaws and operating agreement. This firm is my baby, and I have an incredible emotional attachment to this institution. I recognized that and hired a different law firm to write the agreement. Emotional entanglements induce stress, and you don't take action when you know you should. When you can't perform at your best, you're hurting your company.

Sometimes we avoid certain projects or deals because there is an emotional tie in and the stress is too high, and we might not even recognize it. Avoidance is a red flag. You're disengaged, and it needs to be reassigned or delegated. It's that purported trial lawyer who never steps foot in court. They will do anything they can to avoid going to trial. If you're dragging your feet to get something done, recognize it's an area in which you need some help.

When the stress is high, there are effective steps to handle it in a way where you can continue to thrive.

Step 1) Come back to your foundation. I keep life in perspective by clinging to the things that mean the most to me. My dog isn't going to care if I win or lose this case. He wags his tail, and no matter what, my dog loves me. Strong family relationships can do the same thing. Your children and your spouse can help you remain grounded.

Step 2) Stay in community. Everyone always hears it's lonely at the top. Indeed it is, and that's why community is so key. Share and confide in the appropriate people. It will lessen the burden. You're at the top, but you don't have to be alone.

Peer groups are great for this. I'm involved in a Vistage group. Consultants, the right ones that you can trust, also provide a great outlet. Sharing is powerful, and it lessens the burden on you as the leader. You are investing in others, and they in you, when you allow yourself to become vulnerable.

If you're lucky, you'll find a great mentor. When they're amazing, be a sponge. Soak in every ounce of wisdom and guidance they offer. When you face a tricky situation, you have the ear and support of someone wiser than you. Don't take that for granted. Just because you're the leader, it doesn't mean you never need a helping hand. The lesson is this: Do not try and handle everything on your own, all the time.

Step 3) Breathe. Literally, take a deep breath. Managing stress requires control of your body as much as your emotions. Controlled breathing is about self-control, slowing your heart rate, and clearing your mind so you can be effective in your thinking and communicating. It's why so many people in high-pressure positions do yoga, Pilates, or meditation. You're in a high-stakes negotiation, and you can step out, breathe, and readjust.

My cadence is very intense. I work a lot—and I mean a lot. My executives think I work an average of 90 hours a week (it's not that much, but I do work a lot). I have six planned vacations a year, and the anticipation leading up to each one of those vacations is a lifesaver for me. Looking forward to the vacation is almost as fun as the vacation itself. Each of them is a wonderful period of rest, and I look forward to making memories with my family.

During some of these vacations, I am available to the office if there is a real need. But for other vacations, I'm checked out. I'm off the grid, untethered from my cell phone, and I don't check in. My mind fully disconnects. I refresh and escape. If you pour and pour yourself into your business or organization, you need a break at some point. It only makes you stronger when you are on the job.

Dealing with stress takes mental, physical, emotional, and spiritual training, and I'll be honest, you have to train to be in this place. It's intense and it's not for everyone. Firefighting experts say that in an intense time of pressure, you default to your highest level of training. If you haven't trained for this level, you're not going to be able to handle it.

Keep your mind clear. Reboot. A clear mind is like your landscape. It's your canvas to Ready, Execute, Deliver. You have to have a fresh, clear landscape on which you can deliver.

Be the Problem Solver

When I'm in the moment of execution, I can rely on my training and experience to finish strong and release my stress.

When it gets tough, people want to flee. Leaders, on the other hand, are drawn to stressful situations. People complain a lot about people problems within their organization. I'm not intimidated by people problems—that's what we're in the business of every day.

The biggest problems are my problems, and I am a leader, so I solve them. Bring me your toughest problems, and I'll solve them. Leaders see problems as opportunities, and that's why they run toward the fire. If you're going to be the chief, you get to be the hero. It's even more fun to make your people the heroes. Being the silent hero, when you're anonymously behind the outward hero, is even more rewarding.

R.E.D. Questions

READY

What's your highest level of training? When the building is on fire, how will you react?

EXECUTE

What tools have you mastered? When the flames are highest, will you run toward them?

DELIVER

After the victory, whom do you make the hero?

READY. EXECUTE. DELIVER.

CHAPTER 8

R.E.D. Culture

Juries are fascinating collections of people who hold the fate of thousands in their collective hands. Have you ever thought about the incredible power each jury member possesses as they weigh the facts and render a verdict? It's why I go out of my way, in every single case, to deliberately, painstakingly find the right jury.

The jury represents the community. Jurors decide on the facts in a case, apply the law to the facts, and come up with a verdict. Staying within the boundaries of evidence and civil procedure, I have a core strategy for persuading the jury.

It starts with selecting the right jury. I work to establish themes early in the case and carry them through to the conclusion. I latch onto themes that resonate with the jury members and stay consistent from opening remarks to closing.

I shine a spotlight on emotional triggers to persuade the jury to connect with or dislike people. I align credible witnesses and evidence by picking the right sequence and people to tell the story.

I have the foresight to expose skeletons first—it gives me the upper hand. You come out with the bad stuff because you can keep the power in your pocket. It diffuses the situation if you can reveal it first.

I remind the jury that I am human. If I stumble or miss something, I pick up quickly with self-deprecating humor. If they can't relate to me, they won't believe what I'm saying.

I'm careful to pick the right people to tell the story, particularly the witnesses up on the stand. They need to be clean and credible. Evidence is the same. There are hundreds of pieces of information you could share with a jury, but it's your job as an attorney to focus on the right things.

The Trial Run

I am comfortable when I walk into the courtroom and there's a reason why—I take the time to conduct mock trials. I have committed to the in-depth process of conducting mock trials before R.E.D. cases for one reason and one reason only—to win.

Science has proven that it is possible and likely that you can replicate a jury within close proximity to the real jury pool. So, that's exactly what we do.

The first thing we do is utilize data to create a pool that would represent the real jury. The data is able to approximate the people at random. We generally pick 36 from this sample group and divide them into groups of 12.

We present pieces of the case and play video snippets of the witnesses. Then, using jury consultants (who are PhDs, psychologists, and lawyers who specialize in jury selection), we poll the mock jury members and ask detailed questions about the mock trial. During their mock deliberations, we can watch the results live from the next room.

We get the results from the three separate groups and we use that information from those mock jurors to pick the best jury in the trial. The information is incredibly revealing and gives us clear direction for how to adjust our game plan. It gives us a clear idea of what kind of juror profile we want, and which ones to avoid. It also gives us insight into their perceptions of all of our players, from the likeability of the lead attorney to their disdain for a witness on the stand.

We make adjustments, and when we go to the real trial, we have a much better idea of what to expect. It's a fabulous preemptive strike.

More so, it means we're prepared. If we can run a mock trial, it means we are really, really prepared, and it's a great dry run.

Is it labor intensive? Yes. I do it to win. I glean information from a mock jury that I could find nowhere else.

Just as I go through incredible lengths to picking just the right jury, you must select the *right* people for your team. Who have you hired? Who have you fired? Be intentional in every one of those decisions because they decide if you win or lose. It's outcome determinative, meaning your people are your decision-makers. Did you leave someone on your team that you shouldn't have? Well, they stayed on the team and now they're disengaged.

Is there someone out there, maybe one of those people with whom you had coffee when you were planting seeds for your business a year ago, that you now need on your team? Don't let them end up on another team.

Once you have selected the right people, you must build the right culture to enjoy doing quality work together. The right people (jury) determine your culture. Are they voting yes or no? A jury applies a law to the facts and ends up with a verdict. Your people will take your vision alongside the facts, and they will be engaged.

If you're the leader and you're saying something that your people don't believe, they won't work hard for you because they aren't committed to where you're going. Their perception of reality is what matters. Juries don't have all the facts. They come together collectively to judge the "vision" and create your culture.

Build the Culture

How do you build a solid culture? First, you have to recognize that your jury is all around you, every day. As the leader, you must be so clear on your vision, have so much conviction, and have total belief that it's a part of who you are. If not, they aren't going to follow you.

The same is true when you're in front of juries. I believe we are going to win, and I expect my team to believe it too. If you don't think we can do this, you can't be on the team with me. That's why I reassign people on my trial team who don't believe we're going to win. It's hard-core, but it's necessary because every doubt is a step back from victory. I don't have time or room for that.

It's a warrior mentality. The people you lead believe in you because you are prepared. You are confident and bold.

When we head toward our trial, we know we're ready because we have already walked through the process in a mock trial. My mindset is clear and confident—I can tell you the outcome before we even get there. That's part of our culture.

The themes of your culture help you carry out your vision, mission, and values. At Goosmann, one of our themes is making sure we're not so serious all the time. We have fun, we take time to celebrate the victories, and we value our team. The way we reward people demonstrates the themes that are important to us. You will recognize your themes by what you honor and reward.

If a company gives people an expensive watch for their 10th year, they value longevity. You send a message to people about what is important by what you reward them for, and that creates culture.

Your themes will take on life when you are transparent, prepared, and authentic. You're going to make mistakes, but how you recover from failure speaks louder than the transgression. Admit you are human to your team. They need to hear it. And when it needs to be said, be the one to tell them, "I let you down."

Just like in a jury trial, emotional triggers play a part in every journey. Recognize the key emotional moments of your employees. Onboarding is significant. Every employee remembers their first day and their last, so get those right with your employees.

At Goosmann, we also continue to invest in the emotional connections with employees at midpoints throughout the year. I do company pep rallies. Our holiday party is an event. It's not stale, and it's not the same every year. It's because I want to create an element of surprise, give them something to look forward to each year.

For example, one year the holiday invite was a mystery event and simply included a Santa hat and instructions to gather at the firm. When everyone showed up, we watched a video about a local children's shelter and then loaded up on a bus and headed to WalMart to fulfill their wish lists. We then went to the children's center, handed out the gifts and had a pizza party with the kids. It was an incredible night, and people are still talking about it. Creating those emotional triggers for your team builds unity and culture.

Culture will stay healthy if you are careful to select leaders who are worthy of leading. If I don't line up credible witnesses for a trial, I risk losing the jury. In the same way, if you don't promote people in your organization who align with your vision, mission, and values, you are undercutting your effectiveness as a leader and the mission of your organization. Raise up and train leaders who will honor and emulate the culture you have built.

Your culture can become one of your greatest competitive advantages. Everyone wants a great culture, but they are rare and impossible to replicate. Cultures are like fingerprints. They are unique to each organization. If you have a great culture within your organization, it will become a draw. People will want to be on your team.

The impact your culture can have on your industry is long-lasting. You can be a disruptor if you have the right culture. Our culture is so different than your typical law firm that we're drawing different talent. Within your community, you can give and expand opportunities because you are growing. The people on your team will be more fulfilled, and it will coach them into personal growth. A great culture naturally pushes people to greatness.

R.E.D. Questions

READY

Whom do you want on your jury? Whom would you strike from your team?

EXECUTE

Are you and your leadership team credible witnesses? Have you prepared to tell your story? Have you built your case?

DELIVER

What's your culture verdict? When employees and customers experience your culture, what's their verdict?

PART THREE

DELIVER

READY. EXECUTE. DELIVER.

CHAPTER 9

R.E.D. Requirement

I t probably doesn't need to be said, but I'll say it: Persevere. If you are a leader in any capacity, you already have, and you can't stop now. Finding a way to win is the ultimate requirement for the entrepreneur. You can't lead if you don't deliver. People will flee. Top talent won't stay for second-best. The best clients don't want silver medals. People want to win; they love winning. If you don't deliver, they'll find a way to win somewhere else.

The Ultimate Requirement

The ultimate requirement: push to level-up and grow as a person. Everyone loves to win big. It's like a catapult for your organization when you can win big. The size of a win is really relative, but the point is to repeatedly win, because once you've won at level one, you must win at level two.

You change expectations and set the bar at another level. The bigger you win, the more you have to keep amping it up and scaling it. That's why you have to personally grow as a leader and improve who you are. You're the lid on your organization. If you don't change who you are as a leader, you can't keep winning. People have short-term memories. Don't be surprised when they ask, "What have you done for me recently?"

Continue to step out and step up as the hero. We all love a good hero. Part of what makes it worth it as a leader is to be the secret hero, to spread the credit and shine the light elsewhere. When you pull off a big win, you thank your key witnesses, clients, and all the people who made the deal happen. You shine the light on them. This is your opportunity to give big. If you can reward them and give credit and recognition, you reinforce that culture you worked so hard to build, and it reminds people why the work was worth it.

The team you just congratulated is vital, but at the end of the day, it all rests on your shoulders. If you see the team operating at 90 percent, how do you motivate them to stretch? You have to muster more resources, make some sacrifices, or do something wild like refinance your house to infuse more cash. You do whatever you have to do. This is what leaders do. Close isn't close enough.

Your results will suffer if you only have one foot in the door at this point. If you've taken the leap, you've made the commitment and you are winning, you will have a leadership team with elevated talent, more clients will want to work with you, and your reputation starts to sparkle. You're the disruptor. Your client and your clientele improve, and your bar for success is higher. You need to be prepared as the leader to do that over and over and over again.

You never get "there" because "there" doesn't exist. You're never fully baked. The journey is never really over, and that can be an exhausting revelation for people if they don't love it. The goal posts constantly move ahead, but you're not going to be burnt out. Stop and celebrate the win, reflect back, and then keep moving forward. This is about the process, and that in itself has to be worth it for you. If you are a R.E.D. leader, you are doing amazing things. More amazing things are expected of you. This is your new normal.

R.E.D. is a Requirement

Living the R.E.D. mentality will transform the way you do business and the way you live your life. Know that you will need to revisit the question, "Is it worth it?" with every bump, every victory.

The answer is that it has to be worth it to be the leader, not just to the people surrounding them. It's great if your clients, your family, and the community think your sacrifices are worth it, but YOU have to believe it's worth it.

And then, you must deliver. It is assumed that you can deliver, at whatever sacrifice. Period.

The ultimate benefit to living the R.E.D. mentality is you will have no regrets. You never have to wonder if things could have gone differently had you really put in the effort, made the sacrifices, executed with preparation. You did.

When you live the R.E.D. mentality, you're building a life and a legacy that is worth it. You're building a better life for other people. You are living your best life.

I'm operating every fiber of my being within the R.E.D. mentality. I am taking a journey to positively impact the lives of others. By the time I'm finished with this journey, all the people in the Midwest will have a better quality of life.

It's bold, it's ambitious, and it's attainable. I'm still planting seeds, building my engine, setting the stage, and I'm on my way. I have asked the question, over and over, and the answer is clear: This *is* worth it. My journey is worth it.

Are you in the same headspace? Because, this is hard. If it were easy, everyone would lead. You have to put everything on the line over and over again. It takes all of you. Everything you've got. Over and over again.

And now, I challenge you to make the same decision and then commit. As much as we talked about your team in this book, this part is just for you. With the right resources, you can hire out almost anything, but at the end of the day there is only one you. You can't hire out your push-ups. No one is going to do the work-out for you. No one else can build your muscles. No one can claim your journey, your trials, your victories, but you.

You've got to show up, be present, and deliver. If you truly want to make an impact, there is no one to deliver your legacy but you. It's serious. It's weighty. It's an honor. Decide that you're worth it. I did. And now it's your turn.

R.E.D. Questions

READY

Are you ready to make your goal a requirement?

EXECUTE

Will you do whatever it takes to deliver?

DELIVER

Have you committed to winning?

Conclusion

I wrote this book for leaders who act with boldness, make decisions with confidence, stay the course with strength, lead with vision, and then activate those around them to become more than they are today. I trust this is you. If it is, you have the vital DNA traits, the drive, and most importantly, the mindset to win.

Now, take the R.E.D. *philosophy* and turn it into *reality* for you, your organization, and your family. Make R.E.D. a mantra, a daily commitment to your team and yourself to win big and be someone worth following!

This means three things:

1. **You're ready.** You know winning is built on a foundation of preparation and always being miles ahead of your competition.
2. **You execute.** Your vision becomes reality by implementing carefully crafted plans and building a world-class team that gets things done.
3. **You deliver.** You know results go to those who are all in and believe every goal is within reach.

Now, keep building a business and life that's always *worth it.*

.

About the Author

Jeana L. Goosmann

Attorney to CEOs and Business Leaders

Jeana is the chief executive officer, managing partner and founder of Goosmann Law Firm, one of the fastest growing law firms in the United States. She is a media contributor and event speaker. Jeana was selected as the top 1% in the National Association of Distinguished Counsel. She advises business leaders who want to level up to… BE WORTH IT.

Visit www.beworthit.com for information on our conferences and workshops. Explore www.goosmannlaw.com for legal resources and to contact the firm.

CPSIA information can be obtained
at www.ICGtesting.com
Printed in the USA
LVHW031500060919
630190LV00021B/391/P